Wh ve to eat my vegetables?

FOX EYE
PUBLISHING

Why do I have to eat vegetables?

Because they are good for you.

Yuck!

Why are they good for me?

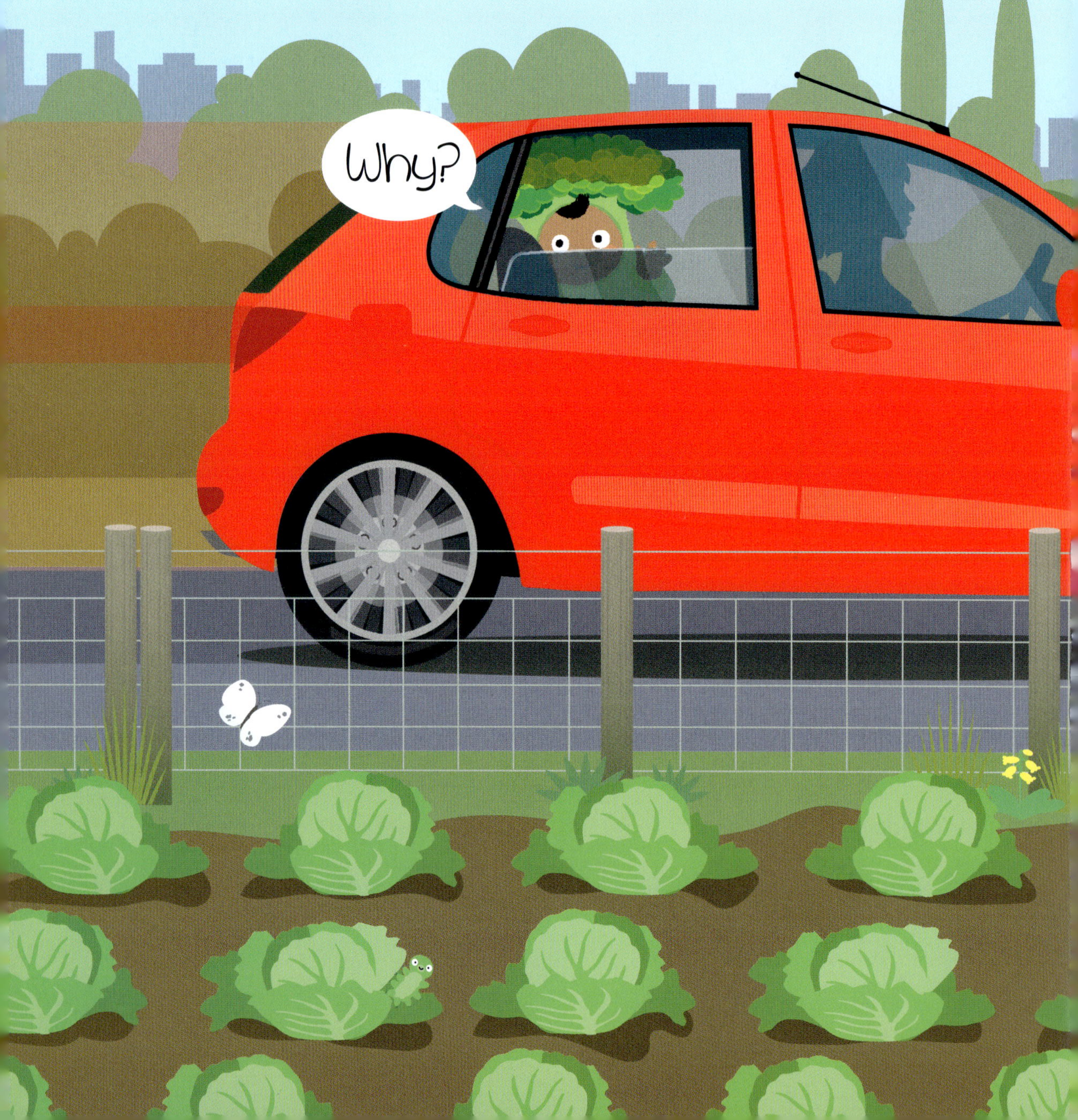

Because they contain the vitamins and minerals your body needs.

Why should I eat carrots?

Because Vitamin A comes from carrots which is good for your eyes.

Why should I eat cabbage?

Because Cabbage contains Vitamins C and K which are good for your skin, blood and bones.

Why should I eat potatoes?

Potatoes are high in fibre which is good for keeping your tummy insides working healthily.

Why should I eat peas?

Peas contain magnesium, potassium and calcium minerals, which are good for your blood and heart.

There are so many
different vegetables you
can eat to keep
you well and strong.

Which vegetables do you like best of all?

Let's find out about Vegetables.

Turn the page over to discover the answers to these questions.

I lik

Can eating lots of carrots turn your skin orange?

Leeks

Radish

Cauliflowe

Asparagus

Celery

Rocket

Corn on the cob

What is the heaviest cabbage in the world?

How many peas are in a pea pod?

Turnip

o eat all these vegetables!

Let's find out about Vegetables.

The answers are ...

I lik

Yes it can!
Eating lots and lots of carrots can turn your skin orange.

Leeks

Radish

Asparagus

Rocket

Celery

Corn on the cob

Caulifowe

The heaviest cabbage weighed over 62 kg. (That is heavier than 20 house bricks).

There are usually 6-7 peas in a pea pod.

Turnip

o eat all these vegetables!

Parsnip

Some of the biggest yams can grow to 3 metres long!

Lettuce

Green Beans

Onions.
Cutting a raw onion releases a chemical that makes eyes water.

Beetroot

Broccoli

Courgette

Artichoke

Do not eat green potatoes, their leaves or stems. They are poisonous and will make you very sick.

How to use this book

You can read this book with one child or a group of children.

The book can be used to begin a discussion around complex questions such as learning why we have to eat vegetables.

The book is also a reading aid, with enlarged and repeated words to help children to develop their reading skills.

How to read the story

Before beginning the story, ensure that the children you are reading to are relaxed and focused.

Take time to look at the enlarged words and the illustrations, and discuss what this book might be about before reading the story.

New words can be tricky for young children to approach.

Sounding them out first, slowly and repeatedly, can help children to learn the words and become familiar with them.

Did you spot
the Tardigrade
hiding in
this book?

First published in 2023 by Fox Eye Publishing
Unit 31, Vulcan House Business Centre,
Vulcan Road, Leicester, LE5 3EF
www.foxeyepublishing.com

Written and illustrated by Simon Couchman

ISBN 978-1-80445-360-5

A catalogue record for this book is available from the British Library.

Printed in China